DISGUSTING FOODS

BY PATRICK PERISH

BELLWETHER MEDIA • MINNEAPOLIS, MN

EPIC BOOKS are no ordinary books. They burst with intense action, high-speed heroics, and shadows of the unknown. Are you ready for an Epic adventure?

This edition first published in 2015 by Bellwether Media, Inc.

No part of this publication may be reproduced in whole or in part without written permission of the publisher. For information regarding permission, write to Bellwether Media, Inc., Attention: Permissions Department, 5357 Penn Avenue South, Minneapolis, MN 55419.

Library of Congress Cataloging-in-Publication Data

Perish, Patrick, author.
  Disgusting Foods / by Patrick Perish.
      pages cm. – (Epic. Totally Disgusting)
  Summary: "Engaging images accompany information about disgusting foods. The combination of high-interest subject matter and light text is intended for students in grades 2 through 7"– Provided by publisher.
  Audience: Ages 7-12.
  Audience: Grades 2 to 7.
  Includes bibliographical references and index.
  ISBN 978-1-62617-130-5 (hardcover : alk. paper)
  ISBN 978-0-531-27222-0 (paperback : alk. paper)
  1. Food–Miscellanea–Juvenile literature. 2. Aversion–Miscellanea–Juvenile literature. I. Title.
  TX355.P372 2014
  641.3–dc23

                        2014006102

Printed in the United States of America, North Mankato, MN.

TABLE OF CONTENTS

HARD TO STOMACH!

You thought vegetables were bad? What if you were served eyeballs, bugs, or brains? You probably do not ask for these foods for dinner. But you might be surprised how many people love them!

FROM UNDER THE SEA

Sort of Disgusting

Totally Disgusting

GROSS-O-METER

Some of the grossest eats are **seafood**. Tuna fish eyeballs are common in Japanese markets. These slimy peepers are usually boiled or baked.

Hákarl smells a lot like cleaning products. This nasty snack is made from **rotten** shark meat. Even the strongest stomachs gag on this food.

Sort of
Disgusting

Totally
Disgusting

GROSS-O-METER

DINNER IS SERVED!

The shark that hákarl is made from is poisonous. Its poisons break down when it rots. Then it is safe to eat.

If you eat **sannakji**, make sure it does not crawl away. It is sliced-up octopus sprinkled with oil. The **tentacles** keep squirming all the way into your mouth.

SLIMY SUCKERS

People who eat sannakji must chew well. Tentacles have been known to latch on in the throat.

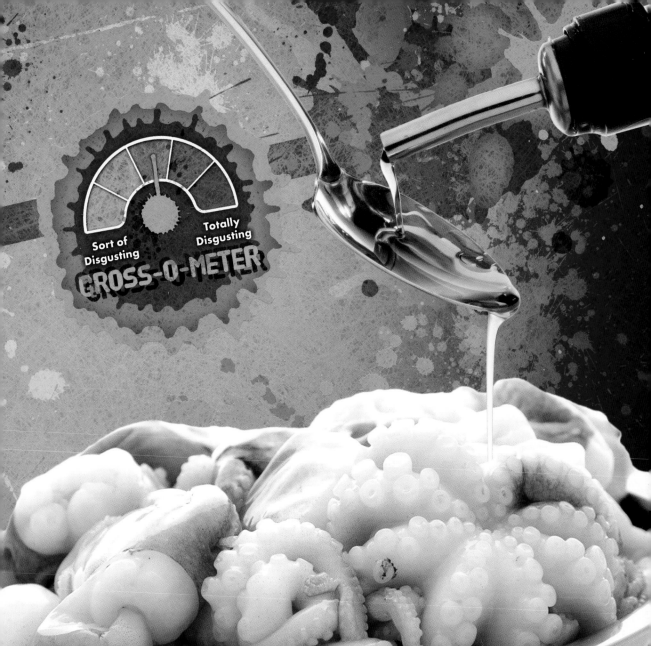

Sort of
Disgusting

Totally
Disgusting

GROSS-O-METER

BUGS BON APPETIT!

Sort of
Disgusting

Totally
Disgusting

GROSS-O-METER

BIG APPETITE

Cambodian tarantulas can grow as big as an adult's palm.

Even **insects** and spiders end up on dinner plates. In Cambodia, tarantulas are fried in oil. Locals say they taste like crab.

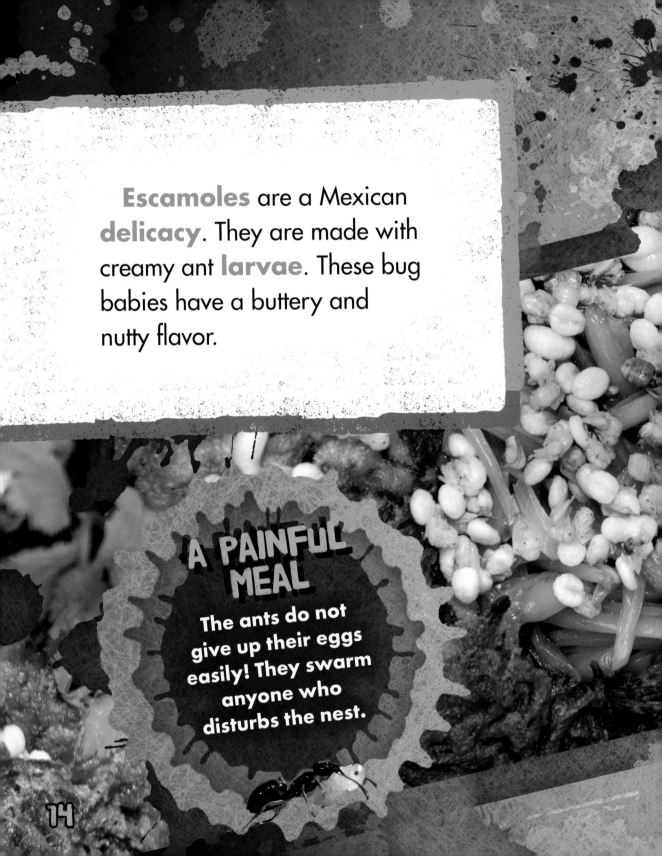

Escamoles are a Mexican delicacy. They are made with creamy ant larvae. These bug babies have a buttery and nutty flavor.

A PAINFUL MEAL

The ants do not give up their eggs easily! They swarm anyone who disturbs the nest.

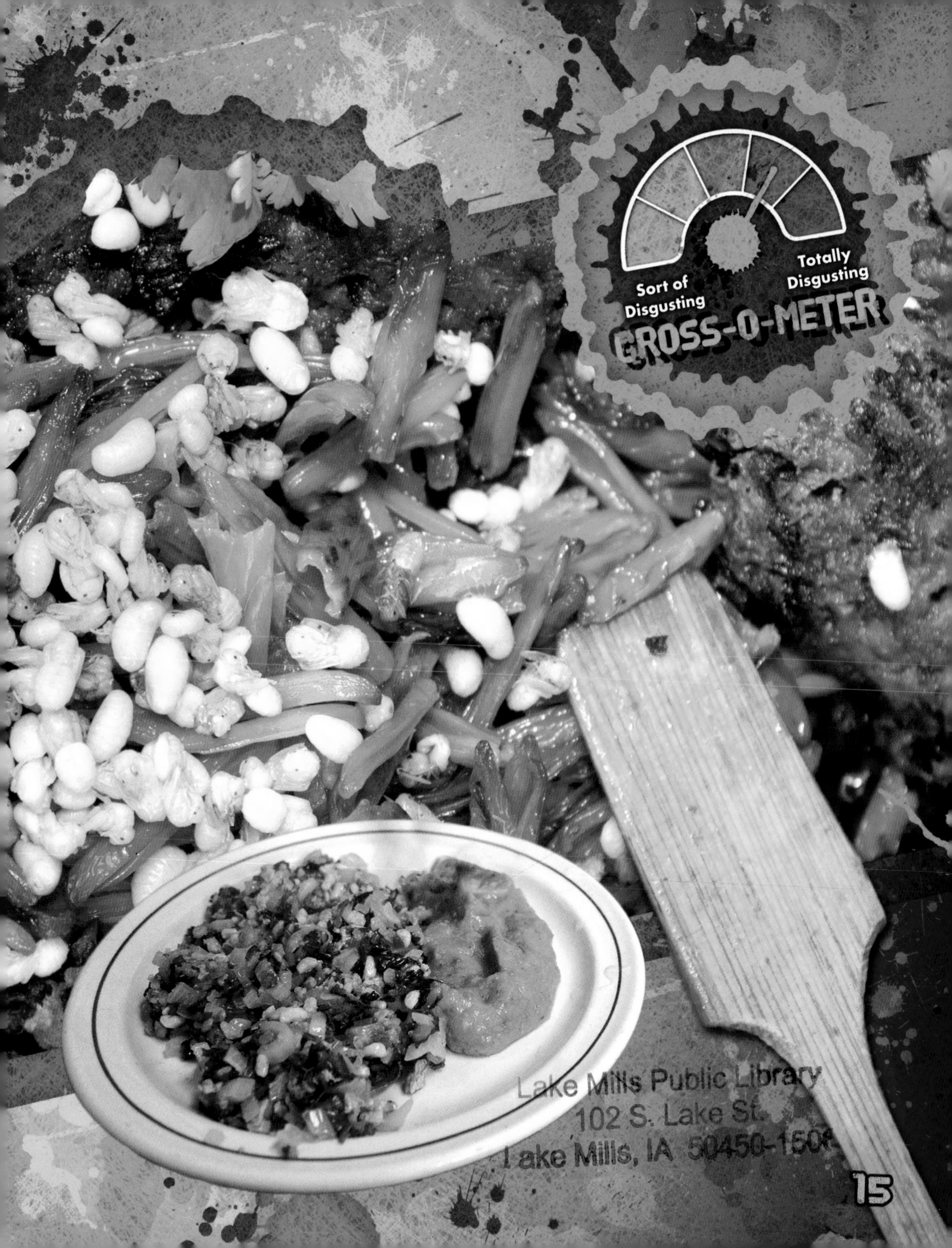
Sort of Disgusting
Totally Disgusting
GROSS-O-METER

Sort of
Disgusting

Totally
Disgusting

GROSS-O-METER

Casu marzu might be the world's most disgusting cheese. First, flies lay their eggs in it. The hatched **maggots** eat the hard cheese. It becomes soft and creamy as they **digest** it. Then people eat the gooey cheese, squirmy maggots and all!

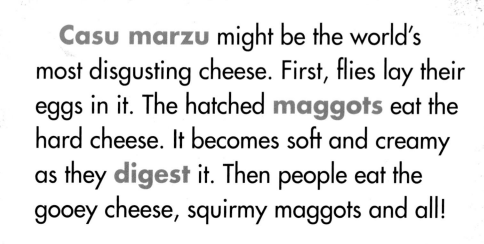

DANGEROUS DELIGHT

Because of health and safety risks, casu marzu is illegal to buy or sell.

GROSS TRADITIONS

Sometimes **mammals** and birds make gross meals. Boiled sheep's head is a **traditional** dish in many places. Imagine if your lamb chops were staring back at you!

Sort of Disgusting

Totally Disgusting

GROSS-O-METER

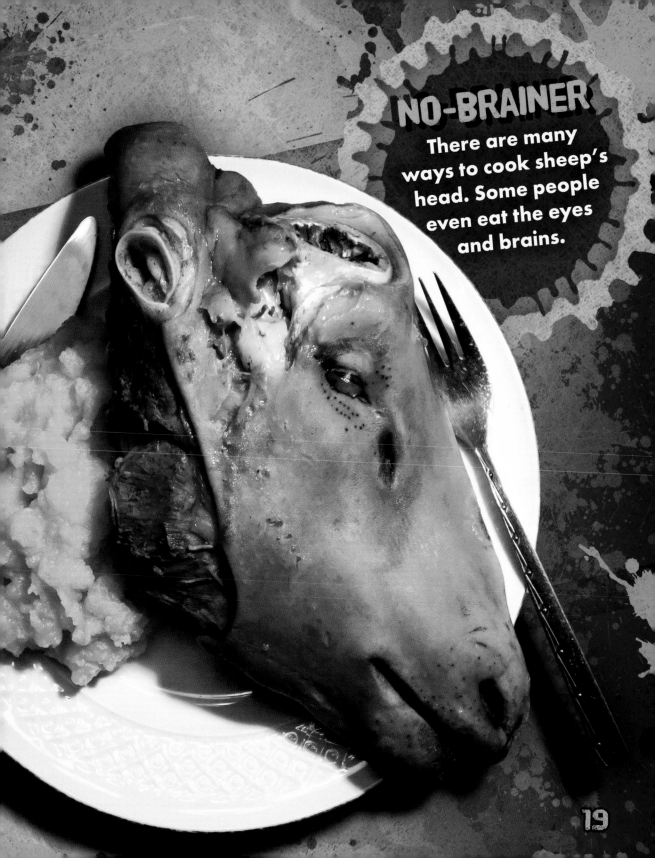

NO-BRAINER
There are many
ways to cook sheep's
head. Some people
even eat the eyes
and brains.

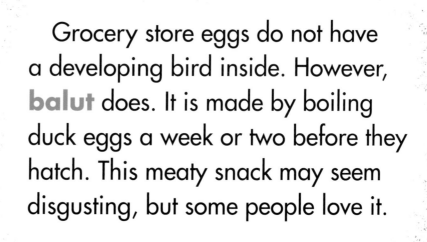

Grocery store eggs do not have a developing bird inside. However, **balut** does. It is made by boiling duck eggs a week or two before they hatch. This meaty snack may seem disgusting, but some people love it.

Sort of
Disgusting

Totally
Disgusting

GROSS-O-METER

GLOSSARY

balut—unhatched duck eggs served in southeast Asia

casu marzu—a cheese made in Sicily, Italy, using maggots

delicacy—a special food that is usually expensive

digest—to break food down

escamoles—ant larvae eaten in Mexico

hákarl—rotten shark meat made in Iceland

insects—animals with six legs and hard outer bodies; an insect's body is divided into three parts.

larvae—insects in the second stage of life; larvae hatch from eggs.

maggots—baby flies; maggots look like little white worms.

mammals—warm-blooded animals that have backbones and feed their young milk

rotten—gone bad from decaying

sannakji—a raw octopus dish from Korea

seafood—ocean animals that are eaten; fish and shellfish are seafood.

tentacles—thin, flexible limbs that some animals use to grasp and feel

traditional—handed down from generation to generation

TO LEARN MORE

At the Library

Miller, Connie Colwell. *Disgusting Foods*. Mankato, Minn.: Capstone Press, 2007.

Owen, Ruth. *Disgusting Food Invaders*. New York, N.Y.: Bearport Pub., 2011.

Rosenberg, Pam. *Eek! Icky, Sticky, Gross Stuff in Your Food*. Mankato, Minn.: The Child's World, 2008.

On the Web

Learning more about disgusting foods is as easy as 1, 2, 3.

1. Go to www.factsurfer.com.

2. Enter "disgusting foods" into the search box.

3. Click the "Surf" button and you will see a list of related web sites.

With factsurfer.com, finding more information is just a click away.

INDEX

The images in this book are reproduced through the courtesy of: Seanjeeves, front cover (top left); wonderisland, front cover (top right); Solent News/ Splash News/ Newscom, front cover (bottom), Scholastic cover; SLP_London, p. 4 (top); Ronaldo Schemidt/ Getty Images, pp. 5 (bottom), 15 (bottom); holbox, p. 6 (top); AlenKadr, p. 6 (bottom); Tim_Booth, p. 7; Ragnar Th Sigurdsson/ Alamy, p. 8; Andy Murch/ VWPics/ Newscom, pp. 8-9; whatafoto, p. 10; Richard Griffin, p. 11 (top); Nicholas Rjabow, p. 11 (bottom); 68/ Corbis, p. 12; meunierd, p. 13 (top); Aleksey Stemmer/ p. 13 (middle); lfmpereira, p. 14 (small); Johnny Jones/ Alamy, pp. 14-15; Shardan/ Wikipedia, p. 16; bogdan ionescu, p. 17; Arnthor Aevarsson/ Getty Images, pp. 18-19; Aletia, p. 20; Marc. F. Henning/ Alamy, p. 20 (bottom); imagebroker/ SuperStock, p. 21.